HEAT

T0362603

Series 3 Number 12

Catherine O'Donnell
Morning Light 2023
charcoal on paper
49 × 77 cm
courtesy of the artist

Catherine O'Donnell's drawings
portray the architecture of a form
that is close to her; fibro houses in
Western Sydney and regional New
South Wales, both the façade and the
interior. Of *Morning Light* she writes,
'At the heart of my practice are my
interests in minimalist structures,
the pictorial power of illusion, and
the pursuit of a shared narrative. By
combining these elements, I reveal
narratives within structures and find
vitality within simplicity providing
a space for personal reflection and
emotional connection to the inherent
beauty of everyday moments.'

PADDY O'REILLY
REDUNDANT

Paddy O'Reilly is the author of four novels, two collections of award-winning short stories, and a novella. Her most recent novel, *Other Houses*, was shortlisted in the 2023 Prime Minister's Literary Awards.

DON'T KNOW WHAT'S HAPPENED but my shoes my skirt my shirt I want them all in colour. I'll throw out all the black and brown, all the neat shirts and flesh-coloured pantyhose, stuff them into supermarket bags and drop them slyly into bins at the shopping centre like people do with dog turds and smelly things they don't want to pollute their bins at home. Bought this purple silk dress – it should have been mourning black but she'd understand – and wore it on a thirty-five degree day. Now it's collapsed around me like a used parachute or maybe a condom darkened with moisture where it's touched my skin and there's no way to get out of this faculty and go home without being seen by

could make a person feel attractive although I remember that time Meg said to me I looked older than my age and she tried to back-pedal by saying, No, I mean wiser, or smarter, you know, mature but not and she trailed off. You'd think I would have been embarrassed – I'm only thirty-eight – but I was snickering inside. What she really meant, and we both knew it, was spinsterish, which might have been awful except relief, that's what I felt, because it meant nobody had seen me and the philosophy senior lecturer pashing behind the lift well after the end-of-semester celebration. We tried to have sex on his desk but he started to spout philosophical logic at me and

the university has changed and we're all rocketing around trying to change with it even though we know they don't want us. What institution wants a thirty-eight-year-old spinsterish possibly sluttish classics lecturer with the cinched belt of the unwaisted and an uncommon knowledge of the Philodemus

9

texts? Definitely not the university that awarded a massive grant to New Modes of Intradisciplinary Auto-Digital Ideologies, while the scarred fragile scraps of work of the rakish yet learned Philodemus, first century BCE, reveal their secrets under infrared light in the hands of scholars on the other side of the world. Maybe I am sluttish but how many sluts can converse in Latin wordplay and wrangle

because natural anger, Philodemus says, can be measured by what harm has been done, whether the natural and necessary goods of life have been damaged by the taking away of life or health or safety. Natural anger begins as a pang, proceeds to outrage, then

couldn't have done it because the photocopier was already broken when I got there, as I told them, but they prefer to think of me as an Athenian *kataskopoi*, a spy in their midst disguised as a mild-mannered classics scholar, or dissembling as a woman on the edge of speaking out. Oh how I would hurt them with a cutting epigram from the wicked Philodemus if only I could caress his charred papyri in my white-gloved fingers. As for the posters, that could have been anyone. I have no idea about design and it was quite a striking

Detonator, that's what I wish I could be. They call her *The Detonator.*

speaking with the Executive Head of Services in the corridor outside her office because she would never invite me in. She has a couch – how did she get it in there? – and a coffee maker on her second desk. Everyone else slouches on their sagging gas-lift chairs in front of cheap pixelated screens and scrapes leftover lunch from dinky plastic containers halfway through the morning before heading out for a sustaining kebab or bag of chips for real lunch. We buy our coffee. Alix from History knows I know she's standing three behind me in the coffee queue but we're playing the deep-in-thought game because we've got nothing to say to each other except

how the wearing of a certain piece of clothing can affect whole swathes of the day. If I had turned up in my usual jeans and shirt would suspicion have passed over me in the same way promotions, sabbaticals and basic respect have? Those *koprophagos metrokoites* in the

always too milky and always tepid. Hi Alix, hi, hi, didn't see you there, must rush. Clamp the arms to the sides to hide the sweat patches. If I could only go home but no, five more hours. Anyway, it's symptomatic of management's desperate paranoia – of their own making! – and a lack of faith in the academic staff that they make us punch our numbers into the photocopier to do copying. Do they think we're stupid? No one uses their own number. Whatever sucker was assigned 12345 has probably racked up ten thousand copies over the last six months. Maybe the dryer in the level three bathroom would dry off my

the noxious atmosphere in that committee room. The Dean's eyes blinked rapidly as though my purple silk dress was blinding him. Lovely costume, he said finally and the other six members nodded too enthusiastically. How refreshing to have some colour in the room, he said, especially at this difficult time. This morning I'd felt like a flower, a gorgeous soft-petalled flower, but in the committee room I turned into a frumpy hippo in a purple costume. I'm not even fat. Sweating started with the agenda, nothing surprising on there so the sweating, I don't know, maybe silk does it. Not fat, not usually a sweaty type, yet here I was oozing out of the underarms, the back, under the breasts, between the legs. Up comes item two and a moment of silence, and I can't stand up for fear I'll

do about these students. Angelo with his pants too tight and the girls all trying to look the other way when he lounges spread-legged on the chair in the seminar room, his small, squashed package no great advertisement. Sophie's hair with its sad little flares of colour every few weeks. I want to give them a hug and let them know that even the Ancient Greeks suffered the same terror and embarrassment of youth. But I can't because they believe I see them only as underperforming brains. They'd be aghast to know that I observe them the same way they observe me. Yes, Nate, this is my new breakout look, thanks for noticing. Are you going to write about this on rateyourteacher.com? Let me tell you kiddo, this is only the

actually no, Meg, I don't want to join the Staff Giving Program, especially when it's unlikely that I'll even be staff next year. Have you considered a Staff Retention Program? And thank you, yes, I am looking much brighter lately. Really? You think this colour purple suits me? It is indeed a feminist colour. On the other hand, perhaps you didn't know that purple clothes were only affordable to those of wealth and high status in ancient

Greece. It reminds me of when I held high status, honoured for my distinguished scholarly career and international standing in the field of classical Greek translation. Worth considering that the Greeks probably sweated plenty too when they

opening the staffroom fridge and finding the seven-month-old yoghurt still there. Oh yoghurt, old friend, I wonder what's going on inside that plastic opaque lid. I imagine colour and textural variety, a vibrant competitive ecosystem. Perhaps your new flora have evolved some kind of intelligence. Could it be you who wrote the new Staff Code of Conduct? Are you in fact employed by the Human Resources Department? So much would be explained by

expect me to write a forty-page grant application when I have five tutorials with thirty students each, as well as lectures, interminable meetings that achieve nothing, pastoral care of students who have anxiety issues (which is almost all of them), days learning the twenty-three new software programs they've decided to make a part of our administrative workload, and spending evenings on my own research. At ten in the evening, all I have left in energy is to lie down with some true crime rather than trying to write a paper analysing the arguments in the new Philodemus texts, which of course I've never seen in the original because

sculpture with the child mounted on the third horse looking delighted, as far as it's possible to tell when the face is crafted from bronze, but a small moment of pleasure on the way in and out through the western path. Professor Cheong from Linguistics arriving at the same time as me on Tuesdays and Thursdays when we nod with the resigned head droop of the doomed and make chat about weather and gardens and how to deal with the sounds of concrete truck deliveries, rattle guns, excavators, saw cutting, core holing and hammering that drown out our voices when we teach

of course they blame me. I was her best friend. I said what I thought about what happened. And I don't blame whoever made those posters but I'll be the one to pay unless

my unfinished article rearing up from its paper nest like a desperate baby bird each time I pass the desk. The author would like to thank her late friend, both a colleague and an internationally esteemed scholar... No. The author would like to acknowledge the important... No. Significant? No. The author would like to express her gratitude to the woman without whom...who tragically

has dwindled away and no one can answer any questions about the future. Only working parties and teams and meetings meetings meetings and proposals and why does all our money go on buildings that look like beehives and have whiteboards too small to write on and computer labs and huge screens everywhere you look showing ads for the university we're already inside or sporting events or some unrelated news content. Last night, thinking about her eyebrows, the way she drew them on in better days, so black and thick and arched as if to say, *Try me*

if I rolled my chair outside on its wonky castors and sat on the lawn near the bronze horses and the child rider and meditated.

Silk dress drying off, the flattened track of my journey in the grass behind me. Bemused and harried passers-by wanting to ask but knowing that the answer might dismay them or frighten them or make no sense at all. No sense at all. And if I had an orange scarf, a detonator-orange scarf, I would

her face when they told us, maybe mine was the same but I think I knew already, whereas she was deep in a manuscript, her brain fused in concentration on that final chapter, the outer world an annoying necessity, her students neglected and fractious, the lime oil-burner scent infusing the corridor with her intensity. One more month, she'd said the week before, and the draft will be done. I'll pay you a thousand dollars to do my marking, she said, and I told her she'd have to pay me a million or two or three but I'd make her a cup of tea to fortify herself instead. Then that announcement, that

might not have turned up in my purple today except changing your life involves changing the small things too. Philodemus's treatise on anger where he compares the debt we owe to people who have hurt us voluntarily with the debt of gratitude we owe to people who have benefited us voluntarily. By the way, do you mind if I call you Phil, ancient one? And just this once, is it all right for me to mimic the rage of the gods? I know you say it is grotesque for mortals to behave that way, but it is a temporary madness. I miss her so much, her snapcrackle laugh bouncing along the corridor, her refusal to

that outside in the air and sunlight the students are like different human beings. Aysha sitting on the grass with her hijab on a

jaunty angle from the excitement of debate and Merlin, vague
starboy of hippy parents, making his first coherent argument.
They defend the notion of democracy even as their own
democracy crumbles around them. All that is solid melts into air.
I wish one of them would rise from the constraints of academe,
mount the first horse and

because I'm only thirty-eight, I'll tell them. A spinsterish,
sluttish thirty-eight, perhaps, and wearing an incongruous,
limp, silk dress, but nimble enough to mount a stumpy bronze
sculpture. Fascinating how the first four or five who passed
averted their eyes. Easier to pretend you haven't seen in the
hazy dusk of a sun-filled day. Along comes Professor Cheong
laughing and waving, and one of my students from last year
giving me a double thumbs up. Ridiculous and happy. First
time I've felt joy since

JORDI INFELD
POET'S POCKET

Jordi Infeld is a writer living on Wurundjeri land. Her first book of poetry, *Certainly (certainly)*, a collaboration with Rachel Schenberg, was published in 2023 with no more poetry. She is currently working on a doctoral thesis at Deakin University on text and textile.

I THINK MOSTLY ABOUT WHAT I'M GOING TO EAT, what I'm going to wear, and what I'm going to write. Today, I'm thinking about what I'm going to wear and how it's going to hold me and my belongings. A snack, a pencil, a pair of snips. Before there is a pocket, there is a pouch. And before a pouch, a hand. But the hand needed to be free. So the pouch was tied around the waist beneath the garments, and a slit was made in the overgarments. Then Lucy Locket lost her pocket, so the pouch became one with the garment, bringing it further from one's skin and closer to one's body.

A patch pocket, with a single flap, bordered with lace, sits at the right hip of Emily Dickinson's white cotton dress. The dress speaks in myth; it says, I have a pact with interiors. This style of dress was known as a 'wrapper'; it wrapped Dickinson in the 1870s and 1880s. Now, the pocket is empty, her dress is wrapped up, and a replica, a dress that isn't a dress, wraps a dummy in a glass case.

It's one of those cold, cloudless mornings. A fine lace frost clings to the grass outside, but it'll be warm and sunny later. I'm inside, holding roughly one metre of orange wool fabric. It is thick and stiff with a thin fuzz that is as rough as a kiwifruit. This is enough, plenty and more, to sew into a three-dimensional form, encasing the arms and torso, with a vertical opening along the centre front (but why overcomplicate things? You know what a jacket is).

Before there is a jacket, there is a pattern. Sewing patterns – so named because they are repeated – are the blueprints of this soft and mobile architecture. I sketch out my jacket in pencil and two dimensions. It will be cropped, squared, collared: a modified version of a 'chore coat'. I cut out two sleeves, two fronts, one back, a pocket, a collar and an undercollar. These are the eight flat pieces of my orange jacket. But where do these shapes come from?

Butterick, Vogue, McCall's – at the haberdashery, purchasing the pattern, I am implored by the shop assistant to line my jacket. She wears an authoritative measuring tape around her neck. A slippery lining will ensure the wool can glide easily over the undergarments, she says, don't you hate it when the under-sleeves bunch up beneath the over-sleeves, or when the skirt walks up the tights towards the crotch? Yes, I say, I hate that.

But before slippery linings, it was the 1920s – Le Laboureur, Carhartt, Levi's. And before that, nineteenth-century France, *bleu de travail*. These early chore coats were unlined, fitted with capacious pockets, straight side seams, and were sewn from a sturdy blue cotton canvas. Chore coats were the outer wrappers of labourers, farmers, or anyone whose dirt stains could be concealed by the dark dye of a blue collar. Now, my collar is orange, but my seams are still straight, my pockets still capacious.

Chore jacket, dust jacket, potato jacket – words move like threads. These are the forms of our travelling garments. These forms endure; they endure thanks to their portability. *Porter* is a French verb that means both 'to carry' and 'to wear'. Wearable forms are ported around by bodies; they are ported to the supermarket, to work, to the bank, to school, on trains and planes. Meanwhile, seated on the bus, the side seam of my jeans runs parallel to the side seam of a stranger's.

Some have supposed that Emily stitched the handy pocket onto the dress herself. In it she'd port her poems, poems which she scribed on pockets, pockets made of paper, in other words, envelopes. She'd open and unfold these paper pockets, flattening them completely, like taking a seam ripper to a garment. After transporting them, Emily would compile these poems, poems on a pocket in a pocket, into booklets bound with a stitch.

The Victorians had a dress for every kind of moment. A frock for every clock! Loose cotton, front closure, no corset – the wrapper was a dress that rarely left the home. It was a dress in which one could work and relax. It was worn while tidying up, drinking tea, and writing letters. And it was ideal for housekeepers when they went to the cupboard, like Old Mother Hubbard (when she fetched her poor dog a bone). Perhaps it should hardly surprise that a woman named for a cupboard would come to share her name with this extremely ordinary dress: the Mother Hubbard wrapper.

Dressmaking is an exercise in unflattening and reflattening space, turning two dimensions inside out into three. You do this with an iron. Somewhere, a dressmaker is making a handful of flat pieces join together, contouring neatly around a curved surface (like an armpit or a crotch) and enveloping an irregular volume (like a leg or a torso).

Since a body part is not a fixed or static volume, there is a constant negotiation with the amount of space between the garment and the body. This space is called 'ease'. Bring your elbows together and the width of your upper back grows. Raise an arm and your torso lengthens. According to the sewing guidebook, I need at least seven centimetres of ease in the bust, two in the waist and five in the hip. These are the three most frequently surveyed points of a woman. A body is only as flexible as its wrapper; a corset converts the body into a rigid form, a large cage skirt puts everything out of reach. But a loose garment can accommodate a woman in motion.

Eventually Hubbard's wrapper did leave the home. Wearing her gown, all about town, Hubbard set off to the baker, to the cobbler, to the tailor. And finally, she boarded a ship and ported her dress all the way to the Pacific Islands. Here, Hubbard helped create negativities – what is freeing can also be oppressive. So the local women made Hubbard their own, and this indoor dress was turned inside out; she was shortened, brightened, renamed. She became the *vinivo* (Fiji), the *'ahu tua* (Tahiti), the *kofu* (Tonga). In Tahiti, her cuffs belaced, her yoke stitched, and in New Caledonia, women wore their *robes missions* on the cricket pitch. But still, Hubbard's pattern – square yoke, full hem, no darts – remains largely intact.

Lucy Locket knew the distance a pocket could go. She is also woman in motion. These women are travellers; they travel in our pockets, they travel in our mouths. A quatrain, a rhyme, a four-beat line. These are forms too! A pattern for a poem moves as easily as a pattern for a dress. Is there anything more portable than the lines of a song?

I decide to line my jacket with a black viscose that wriggles on the diagonal and dances on the scissors. It's slippery, like the assistant suggested. I sew crooked seams and assure myself they won't be seen. A tiny patch pocket on the inner lining to hold something close. A pocket invents a space. So does a cupboard, and a locket. The fold is a revelation; this is what the hinge envies. A pocket says yes to inside, outside.

I lay, I pin, I cut, I fuse, I place, I baste, I press, I fold, I clip, I trim, I pull, I turn, I open, I stitch, I pinch. I join all my pieces together with stitches, a series of small, textured hyphens, running along the edge of the fabric. With wrong sides together, the lining is inserted and the entire jacket is turned right side out and birthed through a slit in the side seam. I put it on straight away and yes, it glides on and off easily.

Note
'This is enough, plenty and more' is taken from Gertrude Stein's poem 'A Cloth' in *Tender Buttons*.

NAM LE
FROM 36 WAYS OF WRITING
A VIETNAMESE POEM

Nam Le's short story collection *The Boat* received the PEN/Malamud Award, the Anisfield-Wolf Book Award, the Dylan Thomas Prize, the Prime Minister's Literary Award, and the Melbourne Prize for Literature. His poetry has been published in *American Poetry Review, The Paris Review, BOMB* and elsewhere. The poems in this sequence are drawn from *36 Ways of Writing a Vietnamese Poem*, his debut book of poetry, which will be published in 2024. Le lives in Melbourne.

[10. Reclamatory: 1]

Me chink but not so fast with
console or condemn, me chinked,
self-chinked in pidgyhole & niche,
notch cranny-hole creft crack —
cramped in here it is, & humid,
is just dey in my mouth, says she,
so ray back on bed, hang back
head, jop jaw, unkink dat magic
passage, straight & true, pink shutup
promise past da jag & glint & hard O
gorgeous gorge for gorgèd dinky
not-too-thinky chink-head O &
O & O O O

[20. Titrative]

Unself-consciously?
Ha ha!
Too late.

[35. Reclamatory: 2]

Moon and jade and silk.   Clichés?

We used these metaphors   Millennia before

The first French matrix   Impressed itself

Upon wet metal   And clicked.

* * *

There are other violences   Of type.

[34. Megaphonic]

They'd rather we be one than many.

They'd rather we be many than One.

BELLA LI
THE PHOENIX APARTMENT

The city is now entirely deserted...
thoroughly eaten by the fire.

Strabo, *Geographica*

Bella Li is the author of
Argosy (2017), *Lost Lake* (2018)
and *Theory of Colours* (2021). Her
work has won the Victorian and
New South Wales Premiers' Literary
Awards for poetry, and an ABDA
award for book design.

I. *La sepoltura del sole*

The city sits on an elevated terrace above an alluvial plain.

The city, otherwise known as the House of Ra — otherwise remembered intermittently as the scene of a burial, now forgotten — is almost entirely deserted.

Of the inhabitants that remain, the remaining high priests are scattered in the skeletons of buildings eaten by fire. Their worship is fervent, though intermittent.

At the entrance to the city, thousands of kilometres from the ancient imperial capital, Rome, the Great Temple bears the scars of Cambyses, Persian king of kings, and conqueror in a long line of conquerors.

Director of a successful campaign in the delta: by all accounts, his death in Syria in the summer of 522 was a mystery — self-immolation and self-creation being, under certain historical conditions, interchangeable acts.

In his account of the city in which Cambyses once stood accused of madness and sacrilege, Strabo describes the plan of the Great Temple of the Sun. The central pronaos, he writes, has *no statue, or rather no statue of human form, but only of some irrational animal.*

One fragment of erstwhile history remains: the obelisk outside the temple, which has the honour of being the oldest surviving in worlds ancient and modern. Its twin having been removed to

Rome under Augustus: a transposition also recorded by Strabo with minimal ornament.

The Obelisco di Montecitorio, also known as Solare, now standing in the piazza of the same name, carried to Rome to be the gnomon of the Solarium Augusti or Horologium: the solar clock of Augustus. Its long shadow points to Ara Pacis on the day of the autumn equinox — birthday of the benevolent emperor god. Bringing peace to all for all time.

In the deserted city of the sun: an animal brings the remains of its predecessor to the altar of the god, to be buried by fire. The form it takes is an irrational geometry that exists simultaneously in all tenses and dimensions. The high priests name it Bennu. Transposed and otherwise known in later dynastic periods as the phoenix.

II. *Le macchine anatomiche*
Naples: the apartments of the Black Prince, circa 1763.

The first study is the incision, always along the fold of the temporal plane. The second is the clone: repeated, and by repetition, known.

In 1763 the Prince commissions the making of two anatomical machines in which are to be preserved and displayed the entire complex map of the human circulatory system. Arteries, veins, capillaries — the involuntary circling of the blood not dissimilar to the revolution of heavenly spheres around a central blaze.

Replicas of the entirely intact vascular networks of a man and a woman are realised, in or about 1763, by one Giuseppe Salerno, anatomist of some repute from the Sicilian capital of Palermo — site of the outbreak of the War of the Vespers some two hundred years prior. Their skulls are sawn and hinged to enable access to the emptied cavities of the head.

La donna and *l'uomo*, whose existence is controversial and whose identities cannot be ascertained with any true accuracy, are installed in a particular part of the palazzo to which the Prince alone has access.

Of the medical discoveries in extant circulation, the following may be of relevance: among those veins that have no true valves — veins of the head and neck; the portal vein and its tributaries.

Legend has it that a third machine, reputed to be that of a child —

An interesting feature of embryology is found in the fate of the vessels supplying an organ that migrates far from the site of its original appearance.

For some, the curse on the occupants of the Palazzo Sansevero, the palatial seat of the di Sangro family, with its ties to the royal house of Bourbon, originates in the gruesome murder of the wife of the nobleman and composer Carlo Gesualdo. Residing in the palazzo at the close of the sixteenth century — *It was here that he murdered his wife.*

A victim of his own extensive and somewhat aleatory alchemical experiments, the Prince suffered the effects of years of exposure to substances fatal to the human condition — when he turns, fate spills through a crack in his neck.

What cannot be accounted for: the reappearance of the body migrated through time.

III. *Nell'appartamento della fenice*
Located behind a false panel in the *sala grande*, which slides open with firm pressure of the hand, the apartment occupies the far end of the southern wing on the second floor, with windows facing both east and west. Each day it receives the piercing rays of the rising and setting sun, which mark the hours.

Several rare and valuable specimens of furniture, in particular from the late baroque, can be found set around a large ornate table, as for a feast.

On the table a selection of carefully prosected parts: legs, shoulders, arms. In the sideboard below a pair of tall silver candlesticks, a drawer of hemi-heads neatly catalogued.

A scene of desolation: *In the ruinous sanctuary of the sun*

In the carefully preserved apartment, a final object of note: on the Louis XIV table is a miniature of a monument standing in a piazza some two hundred kilometres distant, originally appearing at a site four thousand kilometres removed. The statue is mounted on a square base, on which the inscription, in languages that can no longer be deciphered, has been faithfully and meticulously altered:

The Golden Horus, beloved of Ra, Lord of Heliopolis who seizes the sky. I gave thee all life and dominion, and all joy for ever.

Notes

The epigraph and italicised English phrases, except for those in the final paragraph, are from:

Brian A. Curran, Anthony Grafton, Pamela O. Long and Benjamin Weiss, *Obelisk: A History*, The Burndy Library, 2009.

R.M.H. McMinn (ed.), *Last's Anatomy: Regional and Applied*, eighth edition, Longman Group, 1990.

Strabo, *Geography*, trans. H.L. Jones, Loeb Classical Library, 1932.

This piece was commissioned for the 2023 University of Melbourne Body Donor Program Commemorative Thanksgiving Service, and draws from materials encountered during a residency at the B.R. Whiting Studio in Rome, Italy, with thanks to Creative Australia.

BELLA LI
THE PHOENIX APARTMENT II

The first study is the incision, always along the fold of the temporal plane. The second is the clone: repeated, and by repetition, known.

ESTHER CROSS
WE SHALL BE MONSTERS

I felt as if I had already entered my grave – my dreary,
companionless but peaceful grave

The Journals of Mary Shelley
17 February 1823

Translated from the Spanish by Alice Whitmore

Esther Cross (Buenos Aires, 1961) is the author of several novels and books of short stories, among them *Kavanagh*, *Radiana*, *Tres hermanos* and *La mujer que escribió Frankenstein*, from which this piece is excerpted. She also edited, along with Félix della Paolera, two books of interviews: one with Borges, the other with Bioy Casares. Her books have been awarded several prizes, among them the Fortabat Foundation Novel Prize, the Regional Novel Prize and the Siglo XXI Narrative Prize. She has been awarded the Fulbright and Civitella Ranieri scholarships, and has translated Richard Yates, William Goyen and Mark Twain into Spanish. In 2023 she was elected to the Argentine Academy of Letters.

Alice Whitmore is a writer and literary translator living on Eastern Maar/Gunditjmara country. Her translation of Mariana Dimópulos's *Imminence* was awarded the 2021 New South Wales Premier's Translation Prize.

IN ROME'S PROTESTANT CEMETERY, at the grave of Percy Bysshe Shelley, there is a tombstone that says *heart of hearts*, but the heart is missing. Shelley's heart is buried with his wife Mary, hundreds of kilometres away, in Bournemouth, on the south coast of England. One grave holds an urn with incomplete ashes, and the other has one heart too many.

Mary's grave is a silent map of her life. Along with her husband's heart it contains other relics, parts of the people she loved, sometimes too briefly.

Mary had four children. Only one survived. Her first, a daughter, died in a sad, cold London cot. Her second daughter died in Venice at the age of two. William, the son born between them, also died in Italy, of cholera or typhoid fever. She kept something from each of them – a lock of hair, a handkerchief – so as to hold them close to her, although they often appeared to her of their own accord.

Mary saw her dead children in dreams and insomnia. Those apparitions comforted and frightened her. Her grief for her son transformed her into a different person.

after my William's death this world seemed only a quicksand, sinking beneath my feet

She had her son buried in the Protestant Cemetery at Rome, but years later something strange happened: *they cannot find the grave of my William*, she wrote in her journal.

Her husband, too, died in Italy, in a shipwreck. The poet Shelley washed ashore, drowned, disfigured by the sea. After he was cremated on the beach, his ashes were buried in the same cemetery where William had been buried. Mary did not attend, because cemeteries were men's business, but a friend saved her husband's heart from the fire and gave it to her. Mary wrapped it in the first page of a poem. She kept it and carried it with her. She went through life bearing these physical memories. She travelled with her relics, her partial and anatomical ghosts, carrying the weight of her reduced, inanimate family on her back.

When she was forty-five years old, passing again through Italy, Mary tried to visit her son's grave. The rumours were confirmed: the grave wasn't there. She was a frail-looking woman, small and very pale. She wandered through the cemetery, asking, searching for her son's grave, but she was unsuccessful, she could not find it. The same thing happened to other mothers. Cemeteries were disorganised. They were full of lost widows, of fathers demanding explanations from the caretaker and the administration. But in her case there was a macabre irony to it: she was Mary Shelley, she had written a book that everyone associated with body snatchers. Cemeteries belonged to her – they were her literary milieu.

Years later, brain cancer claimed her entire body. Back pain debilitated her, and she gradually lost sensation until she could feel nothing, not even pain. One day she was writing a letter and the words began to come undone on the paper, no longer under the control of her hands. She eventually stopped speaking, but before she did she said she wanted to be buried with her parents in London, in St Pancras Cemetery.

Sometimes it is difficult to meet a loved one's dying wishes. Bureaucracy gets in the way, or there are practical obstacles. Mary was instead buried in Bournemouth, in the south of England. In time, though, her parents' coffins travelled to her. She now shares a grave with her mother and father, her one surviving child, and her daughter-in-law. She is buried with them and with the belongings found locked in the drawer of her writing desk.

Inside the desk they found papers, a book of notes she made with her husband, her husband's heart – wrapped in the first page of the poem 'Adonais' – and relics of her children.

Beneath a simple marble tombstone, the body of the woman who wrote the story of the monster made of corpses presides over a bleak family gathering. Her tomb is almost a miniature cemetery.

The grave of Mary Shelley is many graves at once. If someone were to open it and assemble the figure of hair, bones and ashes they found there, they would encounter not a regular human body but a different creature altogether; something like a monster.

—

...the demoniacal corpse to which I had so miserably given life
Frankenstein; or, The Modern Prometheus

The body is enormous: eight feet tall. The wrinkled yellow skin barely conceals the muscles and arteries beneath. The lustrous hair is black, straight; the teeth ivory-like. The eyes are glassy, almost transparent, a dirty white. The lips are thin and dark.

He resembles a corpse reassembled by medical students after a dissection, in order to restore some measure of dignity before its burial. The students would fill in the eye sockets with glass. Wood replaced missing bone. Archaeologists have found strange creatures buried on the grounds of hospitals – grotesque bodies, like his.

His countenance is one of disdain and malice, but also bitter anguish. He possesses an unearthly ugliness. His vast hands look like the hands of a mummy. Every gesture is inspired by some uncontrollable passion. He shrieks in diabolical desperation. He has no name. Frankenstein calls him devil, fiend, animal, object, murderer, depraved wretch, filthy dæmon, vile insect, being, creature, monster.

Despite his sutures and his colossal size, the monster has an athlete's agility. He moves with superhuman speed. He scales a piny mountain with ease. He swiftly escapes his pursuers. And he can be silent, subtle. He watches sleepers without waking them. He fears no one. *Persecuted and tortured as I am and have been,* he says, *can death be any evil to me?*

Nonetheless, the monster cleaves to life: *Life, although it may only be an accumulation of anguish, is dear to me, and I will defend it.* This tenacity is what allows him to survive the most unliveable conditions. His resistance is frightening. Hunger, thirst, cold, isolation, hate, the fact that he has no name – nothing can wear this being down, nothing can drive him to suicide. His life force is invincible. So much has been said about death, but here is something worse: life that fears nothing, not even death; life that insists on enduring despite everything, justifying every means along the way.

Yet, there is something even more monstrous than the sum of features and aptitudes animated by that dogged life force, bursting forth in the monster's gaze, in his wild gait, in his clinical logic. Frankenstein's descriptions of him are incomplete. This demoniacal corpse possesses human traits. He represents a kind of civilised barbarism. This is what makes him so terrifying.

The monster reads literature (Goethe, Milton, among others). He speaks like a Rousseauian. He is moved by books and music. He finds pleasure, too, in strangling a child. A bestial monster would be more reassuring than this sophisticated criminal who, with his fine tastes, is nonetheless capable of murdering innocents without batting an eyelid. This killer is no beast – quite the contrary.

Compared with other monsters, Frankenstein's is rather boring. He talks a lot. He is emotional, discursive, proffering explanations and justifications. He manages to convince himself that his are crimes of passion: he kills because no one loves him, he kills for revenge, he kills to protect himself from the pain caused by the existence of others. He is at once isolated from society and a product of it, criticising it from the margins because he knows it from the inside.

He is a romantic monster. Like the typical hero of romantic literature, he wants something intensely. When asked what he wants, he requests a friend, a companion. He does not fall in love platonically. If that were the case, he would have fallen in love with a woman – perhaps with Elizabeth, Frankenstein's bride. But he wants true companionship, he wants someone like him; he is practical to a fault. He promises that if his wish is granted he will leave humans in peace. This seems like a fair trade. A lesser monster would have lusted for glory, or, failing that, the destruction of the world, but this monster asks only for a partner.

His attitudes are unmistakably, miserably human. He spies on people. After watching a desperate man invoke his dead loved ones at the foot of their tomb, he laughs. He is insecure, choosing to reveal himself only to a blind man – he knows how hideous, how frightening his form is. He is also prudent, realistic. He is the strangest monster that ever existed.

Like many of the characters in Mary Shelley's novel, the monster is condemned to solitude – the worst punishment there is, it would seem. Everyone fears solitude: Walton, Frankenstein and the monster all speak of it, but it is the monster who suffers from it most keenly. He approaches people in search of a friend, only to have them flee from him in horror. He is the first and last of his species. Worse than that: he doesn't even have a species. In this sense he is not like a man at all, because he has no equal. Others might be lonely, but he is truly alone.

When the monster complains to his maker, convinced of his own victimhood, he inspires not fear but disgust. Indeed, the word most frequently associated with his presence in the novel is *horror*.

My form is a filthy type of yours, he says, *more horrid even from the very resemblance.*

This demoniacal corpse grows frustrated. He recounts his life story (though no one has ever asked him to). He becomes an unshakeable burden to Frankenstein. Frankenstein does not fear the monster; he rejects him.

If the monster did not look the way he did, would he still be a monster? The monster himself acknowledges that it is impossible for men to be kind to him, because *the human senses are insurmountable barriers to our union.* What would happen if those barriers were eliminated? Could a human befriend a monster if he looked presentable enough? What would happen if, as well as giving his monster life, Frankenstein had given him cosmetic surgery?

Mary Shelley shows us the monster's living form, but not his corpse. After farewelling the body of his creator, the monster leaps from the cabin window of the ice-bound ship.

He was soon borne away by the waves and lost in darkness and distance.

The monster disappears. His lifeless body, were it recovered, could have been dissected. His corpse could have spoken. Understanding how he was made might have meant that he could be unmade. But without a body, an autopsy is impossible.

The story takes pity on the monster's body, letting it instead be carried into a sea of ice. It can only be described as it was when it lived, and even then only in glimpses, in fragmentary impressions. The reader is like a witness trying to describe the features of a criminal to a composite artist; the resulting sketch will only ever be a crude approximation of the original, forever incomplete.

In disappearing, the monster eludes, too, the indignities of the marketplace. His freakish corpse would have fetched a fortune among collectors. In his review of Mary Shelley's novel, Sir Walter Scott mused that one Mr Polito, then proprietor of the Menagerie at Exeter Change, *would have been happy to have added to his museum so curious a specimen of natural history.*

But the remains of this particular monster belong to no one.

MARYAM NAZARIAN
SIX POEMS

Translated from the Persian by Arash Khoshsafa

Maryam Nazarian is an Iranian poet and the founder of the Omid Poetry Workshop. In 2011 she published a poetry collection, *The Old Flags of Peace*, a work of anti-war literature that offers a unique perspective on the prevailing traditions and the status of women in Iranian society. Her work appears here for the first time in English translation.

Arash Khoshsafa is an Iranian writer and translator, and a PhD candidate in English literature at the University of Malaya in Kuala Lumpur, Malaysia.

One

I've set the breakfast, the kisses, and the keys on the table.
Please, forgive me
if I find freedom more pleasant than your love.

Two

The one who invented prisons
is also the inventor of freedom.
And dreams were such invisible seeds in the heart.
I'm standing right before you;
Shoot my dream if you can

Three

I fear
The day
My son
Fills his colour pencil case
With bullets
And comes back from school every day
With one more missing finger.
Drop your gun in the river;
The water knows how to deal with iron,
Like the way your absence treated me.

Four

My dear child,
I should not have been a poet,
But a painter
So that I could paint you on many canvases:
Red in a tulip field,
Golden cluster on a wheat farm.
But I would deepen the night
With your black eyes.
Even when a whole crowd disappointed death,
You were the peace,
But we did not realise it.
After you raised your hand,
That the bullet should not have been fired,
The soldiers should have returned home,
The war should have withdrawn to museums
Only to upset the cameras.

Five

She used to hang herself on a clothesline,
Just beside her dress,
Her scarf
And her stockings
Until the wind would blow
And pass through her skin,
Her flesh,
And her veins;
Until she reaches a vineyard
In which a man buried its sap under his basement centuries ago.
Then the wind would get in her hair,
Her hands,
And her feet
To take her to the battlefields.
Then the soldiers would get drunk,
Whistle through cartridge cases,
Generals dance with their guns,
And the world would sink to peace,
For just a moment.

Six

Blackboard
Is a brain-dead tree,
Write I LOVE YOU on it,
And see how it will bloom.

STEPHANIE RADOK
INVENTORY 2020

Stephanie Radok is a writer and artist living on Kaurna country. She worked as an art critic and editor with *Artlink, Artlink Indigenous* and *The Adelaide Review*. Her books *An Opening: Twelve Love Stories About Art* – which was longlisted for the inaugural Stella Prize – and *Becoming a Bird: Untold Stories About Art* were published by Wakefield Press. Her work is in the collections of Geelong Gallery, the National Gallery of Victoria and the National Gallery of Australia.

January

1. Caught like a child with the alphabet in my hands.

3. The past is very present.

4. A certain structure to a day with the quiet goal of developing own work for own sake and other possibilities.

5. What is kept for memory's sake. Are there other ways to keep things?

6. Shedding the past/creating the present/shaping the future.

7. At the beginning of the year or even before, we believe in lists and order, we will grasp the year, and our lives, firmly and conclusively, place it in columns in a book where it can be added up and reviewed, the cost of this, the value of that, the day that something happened. But the year slides in and on like a breeze under a door and refuses to be held.

8. Reading about the lives of others helps us to face our own.

11. Do more drawing. Weed maps again? Inventory – birds, weeds.

12. This side of nowhere – all that I am not.

14. Sometimes we begin at the beginning, sometimes at the furthest point from it.

15. Consider how you spend your time.

18. Last night a green horned bug on the bed, today a terrific matte grey-black beetle at the tank, and a big cockroach on the table. And in the park just when I said to Eno I am seeing creatures everywhere – a baby owl sitting on the ground at the base of a tree.

20. What has never been sorted, what is kept for memory's sake, are there other ways to keep things? Are there ceremonies for departing things?

22. Inner toad, inner clown. Haha.

24. A bumper year, a prodigal year/a year of plenty in grapes and quinces.

25. What is this thing they call Covid – a new plague, an epidemic? Will my street be decimated? Will the front doors be left open as the bodies are removed and the possums move in?

30. A walk, an excursion, an essay, an exorcism.

February

2. The dog's breathing is like a cathedral, a forest floor among trees, a shape inside which I can breathe and sleep softly protected from everything. The dog's body is hot like soup. In resting against it a peace enters me that is like the calm sun at noon.

3. There are plenty of words, no shortage of words.

4. We must find our own consolation, constellation. I speak of the sea and each of us being a boat.

5.   Don't you love it when you open a book and the words you read connect with a conversation you are having in your head?

7.   *Competence is the enemy of art.* Michelle de Kretser, *The Lost Dog*

9.   Every day there is a new reason not to be working. Today it is humidity and the dog.

13.   Poverty-garden – of vegetables and herbs – to teach people what their parents might have taught them but didn't. Poverty – about having less, choosing carefully, being thoughtful...

14.   I wake up to the scent of the night leaving its sweet darkness, and the words of Nietzsche – *out of chaos you will give birth to a dancing star.* Kookaburras laugh in the distance – hoohoohaha. We walk out to see the full moon high in the pale sky, fading stars and clouds full of bears. There is one that looks like you, it looks like you.

15.   Being dutiful, devoted, trying to do the right thing.

17.   Waldorf salad, red lentil soup with pomegranate molasses, baba ganoush.

18.   Invitation to submit a poem to 'Raining Poetry' by 15 March. Theme is 'Precarity', parameters – no more than four lines, up to fifty characters per line.

19. *Aufgabenblatten*/Task sheets
I am not learning German but taking bits from memory and reading to sound out. And any other language too. Who owns the words after all?

20. None of us think we will get old. Or die. Tickling stories.

21. *Nadie se conoce – Nobody knows himself* is an etching from Goya's *Los Caprichos* series. It shows figures in masks and costumes, and refers to the all too frequent self-deception and pretences of people. And indeed to the lack of self-knowledge that we all have. I love the brevity of the statement. It is tossed off, gloomy, philosophical, bitter.

A trip to the library turns up Robert Hughes's book on Goya where I don't find what I am looking for but find something unexpected and heartening that I haven't ever encountered before. It's a charcoal drawing of a very old man with long white hair and beard in a long robe and with an alert mouse-like face, probably a self-portrait of the artist, walking carefully with two sticks. In the corner the words *I'm still learning* – in Spanish – *aún aprendo*. The drawing was made when the artist was around eighty years old.

Apart from his expressive drawing and examination of human folly, tragedy and disaster it is Goya's use of words to comment in and on his own work that fascinates me. Not limited to pictures the artist speaks, he is sometimes ironic, sometimes poetic. He is a voice as well as an image maker.

He also said: *There are no rules in painting.*

21. Hokusai was struck by lightning at fifty and began his life

again. Or so the story goes. His famous words describe his life as an artist.

From the age of six, I had a passion for copying the form of things and since the age of fifty I have published many drawings, yet of all I drew by my seventieth year there is nothing worth taking into account. At seventy-three years I partly understood the structure of animals, birds, insects and fishes, and the life of grasses and plants. And so, at eighty-six I shall progress further; at ninety I shall even further penetrate their secret meaning, and by one hundred I shall perhaps truly have reached the level of the marvellous and divine. When I am one hundred and ten, each dot, each line will possess a life of its own.

23. What you thought was passing/casual was your life. And a particular red purple near a blue hillside that seemed to reflect you.

27. *Denkbilder*/Thought pictures
Last night in the almost dark I picked a Cécile Brünner rose and saw that a young praying mantis had stepped onto my hand with it – I placed my hand close to the bush so it could step back and it did. Could barely see it but looked again and we exchanged glances before it went on its way. And I remembered when my dad took a photo of a very big one carefully held on my mum's hand and it bit her and she screamed loudly. He always took a long time focusing when taking photos.

29. My relationship with brush painting started a long time ago when I bought a traditional inkstone, a stick of ink and a bamboo-handled brush at an art supply shop and went on

because it suits me. It is expressive and immediate, drawing and writing together.

I didn't want to be a writer – I was always a writer. From early on my parents said that I must have kissed the Blarney Stone even though they knew that I hadn't been to Ireland. My mother's father was Irish but I never met him. Nor did she really.

March

4. Songs without words. The birds are in the garden watching me. What are they saying? The same things, over and over.

5. We are all on an edge, an edge where we cannot stop. Is there a story, what's the story?

6. The less you have the less you get – superannuation.

7. This is where we begin.

8. *Spend more time listening to birds* is the title of my etchings of birds in pairs. It is the expressions in their eyes and bodies that are most important. The slightest shift of line or dot moves their faces from surprise to suspicion.

11. Each of us is as simple as sand, here a look, an eye, there a touch, a word, the eyes touch, the words look, as simple as sand.

13. Fringe concert Steve Reich's *Music for 18 Musicians* at Elder Hall creates a certain space – pulses of sound/thoughts of a life lived/unlived/examined/unexamined.

14. You and your inadequate tail – words for Eno. To think that this, the disregarded everyday, the aggravating dog and his hunger, the chaos of the week, and the world, might one day be precious treasure, a memory of ordinary peace. So I photograph the crowded mantelpiece and the dog with his too short tail, his comma. I sometimes say he is the comma to my sentence. One day we might/I might remember this ordinary day and night as extraordinary, a blessed calm moment of snore and socks and clean sheets and sleep.

15. Beach walk, paddling calm and deep breathing of salt and seaweed air, then bitten by a crab on my right heel! On the way home I buy prawns, fish and calamari to cook.

16. Dream
In an exhibition I take a soft green crayon from my pocket and start drawing on the yellow and white canvas hanging on the wall. I shock myself and stop. I think well no one will know it's me and look at the crayon and put it in my pocket. Then keep walking around but keep popping back to look at what I have done.

17. We are waves of the same sea, leaves of the same tree, flowers of the same garden. Seneca

These words were written on boxes of masks donated to Italy by China. Quarantined by the epidemic in Italy, people are singing to each other from their balconies. The skies and sea everywhere are empty of people, for a while anyway. This moment of poetry and fellow-feeling and significant change – will it last? The dream of a planet without people.

18. Shelter in place. In time of plague...brightness falls from the air.

In Venice the canals are clear.

19. The trick is – there is no trick.

20. Sometimes it seems as if everything I have done is ragged and half-finished. How to get on and do the secret work.

21. In the cool of the morning – gardening.

A Journal of the Plague Year. I have a fragile ancient copy of this book by Daniel Defoe – is this a good time to finally read it or just think about its title? What needs to be done? What can be done?

22. Doris Lessing's *Memoirs of a Survivor* – is it here somewhere? Will it help?

23. What do you love? What do you long for? The work that you want to make is to be ecstatic and you don't get there through craftsmanship.

24. Painting is an act and all the planning in the world doesn't do it.

25. With Covid we are suddenly thrown into history which we had sort of hoped to avoid. The changes my mother, her mother and her mother lived through were many so why should my life be any different.

26. Dark night of the soul/or the soil. Night soil. Dante – *in the midst of life I came to a dark wood.*

28. Eno likes Bach, he says you say Bark.

29. You might die this year. Are you ready?

Things just got real, very real. People you know might die this year before their time.

Thinking of having a fire and cooking chevapchichi, tzatziki and potato salad. Will the street be like Pompeii – full of empty houses? I haven't seen toilet paper for sale for at least a fortnight. It is alternately good to be me and full of despair.

30. To get through this – reading a first-aid book, should attend to advanced care directive. Being mortal – tsk. Knocking on Heaven's Door. Playgrounds – locked gates – how to explain to Eno.

31. There's all that holding back and waiting. And all the letting go that needs to be done. You are not your pain, your past or your emotions. Maybe. Maybe not.

April

2. Prepare to die – what needs to be done? Pea soup, herrings, roast potatoes.

3. I see the importance of doing things with your hands, a balance of thought and sensation. The toilet paper goes in an hour, they say it is delivered to the supermarket at night.

4.   Doing vs. thinking, body vs. mind, or both at once somehow. Dandelions, eggs and bacon.

5.   Meaning of the name Radok is joy. Where did I find that? Can't locate it again. Was it a dream? Choir makes me think of school or kindergarten – people's singing faces look as if they are trying to be good, like virtuous children. Should we even be singing in a group?

6.   Sometimes a sensation of lightness. What is this moment? Geography – drawing and words. Geo – earth, graphy – drawing. Drawing the earth.

7.   Need to eat an apple a day – a carrot too. And look for toilet paper. Eno is training me to never leave him. Roast chicken legs with fennel seeds and potatoes.
       The end of the world as we know it in four weeks?! Whew.

8.   People are free (almost) to buy all the toilet paper. History herstory are spaces to think. Lévi-Strauss famously said of animals that they are *good to think*. Contrast your own history/ museum with the bigger one. Proofreading is full of thinking. The past is bright in objects – meaning? A lightness, a lyricism, the writing casts a bit of a spell. Sky-hills.

9.   Common sense that's no longer common.

10. Good Friday – friends around a fire in the backyard, eating, drinking, talking, feeling good. The sky is a white net of clouds.

11. NBN installation. Falafel, tahini, coleslaw.

12. How does a bird stand? Alert – legs wide.

13. Seven impossible tasks. The lists go on and on.

14. Painting is ecstatic – the ecstasy of paint.

15. Roast lamb, garlic, rosemary, honey, potatoes. Snails are company, companions, consolation.

A dream
The toilet is blocked and I must deal with it – I realise I need to probe with the brush and hoick out roll after roll of unused toilet paper.

16. Writing – often cursory, too cursory, sometimes lyrical – using language like paint.

18. We walk up the street, turn the corner and smell water in the air. And collect a monarch butterfly that is somehow stunned but not quite dead. It sends a really strong buzz of something like electricity into my hand. The life force. And flies away.

20. A palpable sense of words offering consolation. Trying to recall the origin of a piece of writing, a group of words going round and round in my head, their rhythm like a knot – some words describing something holding 'such specific character of time and place'. Maybe I will remember it one day. Or relocate it.

21. I feel like the garden is wrapping itself around me. I am gently shaping it and it me. Is it more scary to treasure your life or not? Letting go of the past but where to put it?

Making artwork that I am calling *Family* – on sheets of thick paper folded in half. I am using green paint to make rough basic shapes of introduced plants, 206 of them drawn from the 1909 book *Naturalised Flora of South Australia* by J.M. Black. On the side of the page facing the plant I paint in red ink the scientific words in the book describing the plants. I paint them in layers so they are only partly legible. It is a cacophony, a Babel of meaning, information, knowledge, blood and sap.

And I recall in the National Library of Australia in Canberra many years ago listening to a Hazel de Berg interview with sculptor Robert Klippel where he spoke of making a vocabulary of forms through drawing. And I remember making my notes in tiny writing on tiny pieces of paper, probably on the back of order slips for books. They may even be here somewhere.

22. We are all going to die, that is one thing that makes life precious. With the new disease Covid some will die very quickly, very soon. Is it possible to be ready to die?

Today we see a couple and their dog who has, like David Bowie, one blue eye and one brown one. I ask can they say hello, they say yes he likes to say hello. The dog's noses touch. Eno cries out. O, a talking dog says the woman and starts to say more but goes on walking.

23. Last night I got up at 4 a.m. When I went to the bathroom

Eno rolled himself up in the bedclothes. Then we had to go outside so he could squat in the garden, and I could look at the stars.

24. Gerhard Richter has a big retrospective show at The Met in New York called *Painting After All* that no one can go to as Covid has shut the gallery after nine days. It can be viewed online. Some works are good with red and green blurry flares of paint though too many are dreary cerebral and banal time-wasters. Some are made from Auschwitz photos – why do that? Why harp on pain and injustice? Apparently the original photos are on show too.

I have postcards propped up here and there around the house and no less than three are of paintings by Richter. Each bought not because it was by him but because it spoke to me. One postcard is *Grosse Sphinx von Giseh* that reproduces a black and white illustration of the sphinx with a caption. It is like a page torn from a school textbook and was painted in 1964. Another postcard is one that looks like a polaroid, a big blurry bunch of yellow flowers called *Tulpen* (*Tulips*) painted in 1995. The third postcard is *Venedig* which I bought because it reminded me of the edge of the sea in Venice. It was painted in 1985. Eventually by accident I discovered that *Venedig* is the German word for Venice. That was a day of wonder. It hangs in the kitchen from a thin nail.

24. A dream painting is not a painting.

25. Four years – me and Eno!

26. What have you been doing all these years? Devotion, work, caring.

A bird sings a note twice outside the window.

27. As usual I wish I had someone to talk to – someone encouraging and insightful, consoling and far-sighted, brilliant and bold – maybe that is why we write. And read.

28. J's birthday – tofu and noodles and French apple cake.

29. When meditating I recall Canberra in fog – blue and red – white fog lying in the street – Mount Ainslie – hills – Limestone Avenue.

30. When Eno and I get caught in the rain on a walk we come home and run through the house from end to end chasing each other, doing sharp turns, sliding on rugs and getting breathless. Even when we don't get wet we sometimes do it. It reminds me of what my mother told me about a dog they had who used to celebrate when visitors left the house by dancing and seeming to say: they've gone, they've gone!

May

1. Need a plan, even though I avoid them.

2. Developments will happen if you are on the/a road. I guess there is frugality and a sense of recycling/gleaning/immortality in it. Drink more water/do your real work. Are you consistent or monotonous?

3. *Leiden* – to bear, to endure, to suffer. I first heard the word in a German song about a rose that we learnt as children. *Röslein auf der Heiden* is a song made from a poem by Goethe about seeing a boy who grabbed a rose and was stabbed by its thorn and must then suffer the pain always.

Muss es ewig leiden – must forever suffer it.

He must have got tetanus. There's no cure for tetanus!

4. Dream

Large ropes of cobwebs in/over a cupboard/mirrors. I must remove and dispose of them.

5. There is some place where you are and where you aren't.

6. If you have nothing else to love you may as well love a notebook or a colour.

7. The ecstasy of paper and ink. Wordlessness.

8. Essays manifestos dreams collections words weeds thoughts aphorisms epiphanies.

9. Autotelic.

10. Everyone in Australia to be tested for Covid?

11. Things to do in lockdown – not done. Work on my Scottish accent. Learn poems off by heart. Cook new dishes. But I do those things all the time. Well not the accent so much. Och.

12. The voraciousness of reading the screen, the seduction of sleep. Images and words. And music.

13. A peaceful evening in the study. Eno standing under the table like a table.

14. Too much thinking vs. doing.

15. *The mystery of life is not solved by success, which is an end in itself, but in failure, in perpetual struggle, in becoming.* Patrick White, *Voss*

16. Artwork and writing exist over time. When you see them arranged their recurring features and preoccupations become visible. Made space in studio.

17. Made more space and vacuumed. Feels good, really good.

19. A grain of madness. Necessary, contingent, sufficient.

20. Herb tea, tisane, decoction, infusion, a light touch. Thinking about what to make for the *Medicinal Botanical* exhibition at the Museum of Economic Botany if it happens – there seems some doubt about that – Covid, people moving and so on.

21. Making lists of plants. Plant use – drugs – opium, hemp, kava, tobacco, pituri, mushrooms, tea, coffee. Plant use – fabric – tapa.

26. *Let food be thy medicine and medicine be thy food.*
Attributed to Hippocrates.

27. Who you are. Who you are not. Mucking around/not knuckling down/need to be nowhere/come from nothing.

29. Waiting each day for that open space where words fall or colour moves like rain across the sea.

June

2. The moaning of life. The archaeology of home.

3. Lovely moments last night in backyard on path a snail with long long eyes out on stalks till Eno sniffed it and it withdrew them – later on they were still short. There were two possums in the liquidambar tree, I thought just one at first but actually two – their ears identical. I waved.

4. People tell stories/make up stories to deal with things/to tell things/to be things.

5. Conversation among friends – to remake the world.

6. To have learnt again that warmth is everything.

9. We are all old now, old-looking anyway. Though I still feel at the beginning of everything.

10. Sometimes a sensation of lightness comes upon me when I am doing my work. Lightness/confidence/clarity. I can see pattern or patterns, multiples, words, the world of silent things. The self-revelation in writing, a voice, frankness, humour, clarity.

11. Who has ever heard of book lungs in spiders? One of the longest running controversies in arachnid evolution is whether the book lung evolved just once in a common ancestor or in several groups as they came onto land. Maybe people too evolved in several groups? I suspect so.

12. I am painting images on paper of fifty foodstuffs – as consumed by me in a week. They are herbs, nuts, fruit and vegetables, and I am making a list of their origins. The work is about an immense daily engagement with botany. In South Australian suburbia food from local farms and from all over the world is consumed every day. Surely this is miraculous. I will call it *The Museum of Domestic Botany*.

I paint their names in red ink over portraits of the food or its parent plant. There is an educational flashcard language learning aspect about them. A device for memory, learning and homage. And gratitude for farmers everywhere.

A medieval inventory – the world as sacred and self-renewing.

13. For a while I had breafkast with a man who savoured every mouthful with attention and ecstasy. He used to say: *you choose how to live*. I guess this is sometimes true.

14. The bed is a boat, a raft, an ark, and sleep is another country. And the dog is all peace, mostly.

15. The things you think about when painting...best to not think too much of course.

18. When you have been squashed for a long time it can be hard to find your shape.

21. A story of sorts, a story of thoughts. The great metaphor of the book.

24. Singing was good. Then the silence.

25. Making artworks makes me think again about what it is to make something rather than talk about it – it's all decision/decision/decision. One after the other. And doubt/fear, complex/simple, refined/raw, slow/fast, skilled/loose...alive and engaged in the moment. Artwork – care/caring/careful to be free/to get lost in it. So amazing to research, find and see a sesame plant, a lentil plant.

27. Why collect the past? Why hang on to it? Must you agonise about everything? Always the big picture. Eno and I say to each other – we all want everything to be the same all the time forever. And, by the way, we don't know where anything is.

29. A beautiful day – all silvery yellow and green.

31. My poem sent to the 'Raining Poetry' project was accepted! Along with others the poem is to be spray-painted with hygroscopic paint in the city in August. The poems can only be seen when it rains or you water them. Who knows how long they will last.

July
2. Today the sunlight burst in every door and window with

a clear calm light, green and softness, silence, leaf-shine and shadow, red stems, yellow leaves, blue flowers.

Maybe because we know a storm is coming it is calmer/quieter/more silent.

3. The koala in the tree is wedged up there. The storm is coming. The deep dog silence that I adore. Gas, dandruff, whining, it's all okay cos there is love.

4. Snail Stories stored up for future reference.

6. A woman in the park tells us we are not a woman with a dog but a dog with a woman. I say he is old and also do you think I am spineless? Clearly she does. We walk infinitesimally slowly as I trail along after him, always attached by the lead, pandering while pondering, stopping and starting, letting him call the trail. After all he is the one alert to a hundred thousand scents not me. And I don't want to tell him what to do all the time. I am thinking of other things.

7. Being here with so much old stuff seems odd and I think helps to make me feel that I am still a child.

8. I do a great line in regret, my hands like bird wings.

10. *Tomorrow will be the same but not as this is* is the title of a painting by Colin McCahon. The words are painted on it. It's not a quote but his words. Curator and historian Justin Paton says he has seen posters and postcards of it pinned up in many NZ artists' studios.

15. Let me be a lighthouse – words upon my lips on waking.

19. Dream
In room we are hanging artworks up. We speak of another time the work was shown and he says I have a photo of you from then. Then another friend and I walk and recite 'The Second Coming' by Yeats.

20. Buy face masks – may as well. Make falafel.

24. A book takes you inside...something...someone.

30. A person is like a stone with layers, crystals and colour. A person is like a tree with branches, leaves and fruit. A person is like the sky with clouds, a moon and stars. A person is like a garden with paths, shadows and herbs. A person is like a home with rooms, floors and walls.

August
1. The dew this morning – lots of it scattered on green grass pointing up. I don't want ten thousand fragments. I have ten thousand fragments. I want to form a whole of fragments.

3. Pea soup, fish tagine, baklava.

4. Where the hills go down to the sea.

5. In the long tunnel of the night we make herbal tea and talk about the stars. I think about healing – the world, the house, my life. Your breath is a palace, your eyes are windows.

6. Writers are like icebergs.

7. On the news an interview with a man in Beirut after the explosion. He says: We've lost our home. We've lost our business. We've lost our lives. We're trying to stay positive.

8. Dream
Rooms in each of which a Hieronymus Bosch work or several in frames. Another room where I keep finding shards of blue-and-white china.

9. Walk at the beach and see dolphins, dolphins.

10. *Go love without the help of any Thing on Earth.* William Blake

11. Thick description, local knowledge.

13. The gift of Eno. From a distance I can see the purity of his face. He looks wonderful today.

14. Watching Brian Dillon talking about *Essayism* in Shakespeare's Bookshop in Paris. An essay doesn't need a conclusion.

15. Dip and celery, soup, pork chop with plum sauce and vegetables – a three-course meal with Helen Garner's diary.

16. Eno gets me to sit on the sofa with him by standing and staring at me. Pretty tricky.

17. This great silence, a ringing in my ear that seems to consume my brain. You are here to make the inventory of everything, picking the past like flowers. Remember Philip Glass in the movie by Scott Hicks saying: *Why are we here? We're here to do the work.*

18. The world is wide but my path is narrow. The world moves with a continual flow while I stop and wait, study old books and boxes of flashing ideas, regret and indecision. The world shifts and stirs with blankets of darkness and rain while I arrange objects on shelves which go on to arrange themselves. There is a silent roaring against the window. I try to find my place to remember where I am, to look after myself and others as well as I can. The sound of the rain, white brushstrokes on loose canvas. The world turns and I follow.

22. Strange times/end times. How many apocalypses can one world have?

24. We are singing and trying to wake neither the dog nor the sleeping children. We are opening the words to the present with our breath and being, stopping time, lighting the dark.

26. I want to catch the flow, the flower of life, to milk the past as if it was an old goat and make cheese from it like my sister who wastes no scraps. I am made of rye bread with caraway seeds, dates and yoghurt, apples, honey, and goat cheese too when I am lucky.

28. Drove up in the hills to meet Melinda Rankin, Director of Fabrik at Lobethal. It is an art, culture and history space located in the old Onkaparinga Woollen Mill. Here they used to spin sheep's fleece into wool and then make blankets and other woollen things. I told her about the paintings of plants I have been making – *The Museum of Domestic Botany* – and she wants to show them in September.

30. My 'Raining Poetry' poem has been sprayed on the pavement island outside Government House. I went in early with the dog and had to borrow $2.50 from someone on the street not realising that you had to pay for parking early on a Sunday morning. Went again with J and this time took a water bottle to sprinkle on the poem to make it visible, grey on grey.

Always knew I was a grasshopper
not an ant
but does the wind
need to be so cold

September

1. Self-knowledge is elusive and maybe also illusory.

5. The hundred things I didn't say.

6. Beach walk hurrah. Two albatrosses. A dog is neither a robot nor an object. Nor am I.

9. Too much self-reflection is as bad as not enough.

10. To see the world in a grain of rice. Handling food – the primal things.

11. Making new work I am calling *Adelaide Wall Paintings* on large pieces of unstretched canvas with a sense of urgency as the show opens this month at Fabrik. Each one is based on a smaller painting on paper or cardboard of part of the garden, very loose, with a sensation of fresco, a light touch. Watery green, blue and bright yellow. And much air to fly through. I did want to paint on the wall but that didn't happen. Fabrik is an industrial space full of light. The canvases will hang beside the vitrines full of stacks of paintings of food, garden tools and fossil books.

12. Domestic Botany begins in childhood. Garden tools are handed down from generation to generation, or lost amongst the plants.

14. Seeds and stories, memory and imagination, the lives of plants and those of people are joined together in books.

16. The generation of the heart of the world.

18. The thing about spring is its familiarity.

20. Can you write and paint?
Can you think and paint?
Can you write and think?

22. Museums are portals to memory. Fossilised books can no longer be opened but are full of quiet moments of great happiness. It's called reading. A fossil book contradicts a book in that it can't be opened but it can be imagined which is often better.

25. I attend Alan Brissenden's funeral online. He was the best lecturer that I ever had at university. Words about him... impressive, wide-ranging. He was called a happy sharer, respectful, cheerful, inquisitive. A lively and intelligent man of wit and curiosity who apparently loved eating cheese with a Barossa Valley red, and annually cleaned his chandelier. He has five grandsons. I once gave him a lift home from an *Adelaide Review* launch. He was their dance critic, I was one of their art critics.

26. The exhibition opens at Fabrik. We all have to sit down with our drinks and have paper bags of snacks so that we do not mingle our breath or hands. We are not wearing masks however. It all feels strange and like a subdued emergency. Has life changed forever?

October
1. What have I learned from *The Museum of Domestic Botany*? How good it was to make the work, to know it would be seen, to have to make decisions. The importance of not overthinking. To be gentle and thoughtful.

2. Casting off. The gestural work.

3. Epiphany is not only revelation or insight, it is also the reassembly of the self through the senses. Teju Cole

8. Prevarication/oblivion/planning/escapism/provincialism/ writing.

9. Black cockatoos – one and a flock. Their languid movement across the sky, their wings, their calls. A lack of solitude, a noticing of solitude.

10. Noetic.

11. The past/versions of it/stopping points/decisions/old drafts.

12. Beginnings are easy. Sticking with something is not easy. For me there needs to be an element of discovery involved.

13. Garden pressing in at every window swelling green and roses.

14. Winnowing, unwinding – writing the same book twice.

15. No internet. Let's call it a hiatus. The air possesses a certain wide silence. I decide to record more about each day. And to seriously at long last make more space around me by sorting and discarding, as well as cleaning and repairing. This is my constant task but really always a prelude.

16. Dream
With an old friend at an exhibition, a circular museum of childhood and at the top of the stairs you hang an apple and it all lights up.

17. Uncovering the past must be combined with the present because retrieval on its own is too heavy a task.

18. *Lacrimae rerum* – the tears of things. I buy a bottle of Italian dry sparkling wine called Dante. He was a writer I say to myself out loud but not too loud in the bottle shop.

19. Through illness a growth in self-knowledge.

20. The light leaving the garden.

21. The past – what was it for?

23. Cameras without film – the act is there – and there is no tedious product to store or view...this is A Radical Idea.

25. Prawns, roast red capsicums, tabouli.

27. Untold stories are about what – the growth of compassion, of suffering, solitude and privacy. Editing the final proof of my book. It's charming/clunky, cute/repetitive, rhetorical/unfocused, archaeological/original.

29. Incantation, healing.

30. You and walls and walks. Beijing – Venice.

November
1. Dream
A 'birth' through a very tight tube to a room with two people in it. How long are you here? I say. This is it, they say. I pull a long cutting – a plant – from inside my clothes.

2. No use taking the great view – need small view.

4. There is an active level beneath language through which objects communicate. Here and there the language is supple and fluid and special. Biffle baffle sniffle snaffle. The work or the life or nothing.

5. By doing by doing. Not what everyone else does but what you do, that frozen, that stuck.

6. Dog is my minder, boss, child. When no dog is around I spend more time looking at other creatures.

10. Starting to make artworks for the exhibition at the Museum of Economic Botany – where *The Museum of Domestic Botany* was originally to be shown. Using fine delicate Zerkall Book paper again and sanguine red shellac ink to paint herbs and then before it dries writing in blue ink right over and through the image so the colours flood together – finding the words while writing – like talking in a dream.

11. You can recycle biros, not birds, biros. Birds too I guess.

12. There is a symbolic African bird – Sankofa – which goes forward while looking back.

16. I have a close and constant companion with whom I am often impatient. He sleeps with his front paws together as if he is praying. His ears are like petals. His back paws are crossed. I pretend he gives me a compliment to butter me up and then I pretend I am cross though anyone can tell that I am really pleased. A small ritual. Aw Eno!

18. Really noticing the difference between morning and afternoon light. The idea of immersion and not knowing where you are going but finding it.

19. Six days lockdown. Hopefully only six though who knows. Eno the musician is always talking about tidying up his studio while listening and putting things together. We often listen to his album *Thursday Afternoon.*

20. Geoff Dyer – on rules for writing – *have regrets every day.*

21. Logic says no more large canvases – desire says otherwise – I have four in to be hemmed at the dry cleaner at Marryatville.

22. Herbs and words. Creating an inventory, a guide. Anecdotes/wisdom/silence.

23. This is where we begin. The technologies, the times we have lived through. The rhythm of words. Cadence. A painting is not a window but a door.

25. Losing the first fine careless rapture for second thoughts and plangent platitudes. I guess you just have to keep going.

27. Peach leaf wine, tapenade, cherries.

28. A snail on the path – slow/radiant/perfect.

30. The story of journals, notebooks.

December
1. I like domesticity/grace/arrangement/style. I like walking by the sea, paddling.

2. In early handwritten books also known as incunabula there were nobreaksbetweenwords, non-naturalistic colours, words as objects.

Cool green silences in the morning garden remind me to breathe deeply, be calm and secretive.

3. The idea of a primer – learning to write.
   Home Schooling – is the title of my artwork from 2017 consisting of two large plaster books on which someone seems to be learning to write or brush or paint in a chalky blue. You see a struggle, a piece of time. Many children are being home schooled now because of Covid.

4. Yesterday morning in studio, in the afternoon some shopping. Eight works on paper – herb and writing. Writing and image, layering thinking.

5. These new works on paper of herbs and writing contain something like automatic writing. The texture and the colour of the sanguine ink stirs me inside. Being stirred what does that mean? Touched in the centre, the heart, the stomach. Every time I see a drawing on stone from ancient Egypt – that red reaches inside me. Iron oxide, red ochre, the earth, blood.

Listening to thoughts.

6.   Story written in bed in head last night with eyes closed –
something about bookshelves.

7.   *That language can multiply itself and form secret and
unusual patterns, while everything is put away in the drawer.*
Ania Walwicz

8.   Realise I have a project. There is the journey and there is the
story of the journey.

10.   The plum tree is a bride.
       And when I stand under its net, its veil, I am one too.

11.   Nothing like illness to clear the head. Today empty I give
myself the gift of nothing and ideas flow in as I sit on the sofa.

12.   Eat like the animals. Which ones?

16.   Song of Eno and S as pirates.

We are ne'er do wells
Who have gone 'round the bend
And are not coming back

17.   Stay calm, be calm. Feel deracinated. My way of working
burns things up. Sketches for wall paintings. Window works.
A work from every window.

19. Lazy soft slow day. Will I begin today what I always plan to begin – an account of what I do and why? A catalogue of works. A new year, a new start. Always I feel like getting going at the end of the year. Well usually. Making pickles and bitters. And writing.

20. I've been having a holiday, a vast idleness, indolence. It might go on forever.

21. An end to procrastination!!!

22. Gaps/gaps, cursory moments to work unselfconsciously.

23. Dessert for Xmas? Drawings for large paintings, pencil, colour, scale.

24. Cards and gifts. Dolmades. Nice cheese, goat and blue.

25. Writing as intimacy. Late picking. Gone to seed. Some of the garden needs to have fallen together rather than being planned.

26. Seeing the value of intuition and the moment. Simplicity and not too much of anything.

Where are the pages of sages? Where is my folder of songs and words? Where are my words? The words I learn to sing and say off by heart. They are here somewhere.

Learn to listen/to pretend/to respond/to be hardworking and not blame others if you aren't.

27. Inspiring interview on the radio with Mavis Staples, and one with a guy from Radiohead who speaks of – *when the songs started coming.*

28. The plan or the plot for the day – out/in. Plum sauce, plum jam, bowls of marvellous plums.

Once upon a time I read a short story in which a young couple painted their house in summer. I could never find it again but always remember it. Every summer I like to do some painting of the house and listen to the radio and enter that dream-space of stillness and hope.

The doorway of a poem/doors opening to meanings. Dog sounds – a light hum or rumble, a completely silent breathing.

The fox knows many things, the hedgehog only one. I like to repeat this sentence over and over. A mantra or a koan maybe?

29. Seeing or focusing on deficits – a habit. Herbs and words – evergreen. A list of words on a scrap of paper, a blackboard, on your skin.

30. Museum of useful botany. Leaves and memory. Museum of herbs – aromatic. The language of flowers. Insistent dialogue. Ways to remember. Words from memory. Words for memory. When you stop watching yourself – that is good.

31. The making of shade.

New Titles from Giramondo

Fiction

Max Easton *Paradise Estate*
Nicholas Jose *The Idealist*
Pip Adam *Audition*
Sanya Rushdi *Hospital* (trans. Arunava Sinha)
Alexis Wright *Praiseworthy*
Shaun Prescott *The Town*
Jon Fosse *Septology* (trans. Damion Searls)
Shaun Prescott *Bon and Lesley*
George Alexander *Mortal Divide*: *The Autobiography of Yiorgos Alexandroglou*
Luke Carman *An Ordinary Ecstasy*
Norman Erikson Pasaribu *Happy Stories, Mostly* (trans. Tiffany Tsao)
Jessica Au *Cold Enough for Snow*

Non-fiction

Imants Tillers *Credo*
Bastian Fox Phelan *How to Be Between*
Antigone Kefala *Late Journals*
Evelyn Juers *The Dancer: A Biography for Philippa Cullen*
Gerald Murnane *Last Letter to a Reader*

Poetry

Amy Crutchfield *The Cyprian*
Louise Carter *Golden Repair*
π.O. *The Tour*
Luke Beesley *In the Photograph*
Grace Yee *Chinese Fish*
Autumn Royal *The Drama Student*
Lucy Dougan *Monster Field*
Michael Farrell *Googlecholia*
Lisa Gorton *Mirabilia*
Zheng Xiaoqiong *In the Roar of the Machine* (trans. Eleanor Goodman)
Lionel Fogarty *Harvest Lingo*

For more information visit giramondopublishing.com.

Subscribe Now
And receive each issue of HEAT
Australia's international literary magazine

Since its inception in 1996, HEAT has been renowned for a dedication to quality
and a commitment to publishing innovative and imaginative poetry, fiction,
essays and hybrid forms. Now, in the third series, we bring together a selection
of the most interesting and adventurous Australian and overseas writers.
HEAT is posted to subscribers every two months, forming a unique, cohesive
whole. Your subscription supports independent literary publishing, and
enables us to cultivate and champion new writing.

Visit giramondopublishing.com/heat/ to subscribe.

Submission Guidelines
HEAT welcomes submissions of fiction, essays, poetry and translated works
throughout the year. We encourage writing which gives full rein to the author's
voice, without the restriction of a word limit. In the case of poetry, we seek
longer poems, or a selection or sequence of poems. For further information,
please visit our website.

Acknowledgements

We respectfully acknowledge the Gadigal, Burramattagal and Cammeraygal peoples, the traditional owners of the lands where Giramondo's offices are located. We extend our respects to their ancestors and to all First Nations peoples and Elders.

HEAT Series 3 Number 12 has been prepared in collaboration with Ligare Book Printers and Candida Stationery; we thank them for their support.

The Giramondo Publishing Company is grateful for the support of Western Sydney University in the implementation of its book publishing program.

This project has been assisted by the Australian Government through Creative Australia, its principal arts investment and advisory body.

This project is supported by the Copyright Agency's Cultural Fund.

HEAT Series 3
Editor Alexandra Christie
Designer Jenny Grigg
Typesetter Andrew Davies
Copyeditor Aleesha Paz
Marketing Manager Kate Prendergast
Publishers Ivor Indyk and Evelyn Juers
Associate Publisher Nick Tapper

Editorial Advisory Board
Chris Andrews, Mieke Chew, J.M. Coetzee, Lucy Dougan, Lisa Gorton,
Bella Li, Tamara Sampey-Jawad, Suneeta Peres da Costa, Alexis Wright
and Ashleigh Young.

Contact
For editorial enquiries, please email
heat.editor@giramondopublishing.com.
Follow us on Instagram @HEAT.lit and
Twitter @HEAT_journal.

Accessibility
We understand that some formats will not be accessible to all readers.
If you are a reader with specific access requirements, please contact
orders@giramondopublishing.com.

For more information, visit giramondopublishing.com/heat.

Published December 2023
from the Writing and Society Research Centre
at Western Sydney University
by the Giramondo Publishing Company
Locked Bag 1797
Penrith NSW 2751 Australia
www.giramondopublishing.com

Typeset in Tiempos and Founders Grotesk Condensed
designed by Kris Sowersby at Klim Type Foundry

Printed and bound by Ligare Book Printers
Distributed in Australia by NewSouth Books

A catalogue record for this book is available from
the National Library of Australia.

HEAT Series 3 Number 12
ISBN: 978-1-922725-11-0
ISSN: 1326-1460